**FOLLOW THE LEADER STORIES**

# You, Jonah!

## CAROLYN NYSTROM

### Illustrated by Sharon Dahl

**MOODY PRESS**

CHICAGO

Carolyn Nystrom is well known as the author of Moody Press's long-lived doctrinal series, Children's Bible Basics. She has written 64 books—some available in ten languages—as well as stories and curriculum material. A former elementary school teacher, she also served on the curriculum committee of her local school board.

Carolyn and her husband, Roger, live in St. Charles, Illinois, a Chicago suburb. As foster parents, they have cared for seven children in addition to their own two daughters. In her spare time, Carolyn enjoys hiking, classical music, gardening, aerobics, and making quilts.

Now award-winning artist Sharon Dahl has teamed up with Carolyn Nystrom to provide lively, captivating illustrations for the Follow the Leader Series. Sharon lives with her husband Gordon and daughters Samantha and Sydney in Boonton Township, New Jersey.

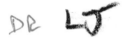
Moody Press, a ministry of the Moody Bible Institute, is designed for education, evangelization, and edification. If we may assist you in knowing more about Christ and the Christian life, please write us without obligation: Moody Press, c/o MLM Chicago, IL 60610.

ISBN: 0-8024-2204-7

1 3 5 7 9 10 8 6 4 2

Printed in the United States of America

"You! Jonah!" said a voice I'd heard before.

"Who? Me?" I asked.

"Yes, you, Jonah."

"What do You want me to do, God?"

"Go to Nineveh," said the voice.

I groaned. "But that's 600 miles, and I'll have to walk all the way!"

"I have a message for the people there," God said.

"Tell them I have seen all the bad things they do, and I want them to stop."

"But I don't even like the people of Nineveh," I shouted.

"I love them," God whispered.

I didn't go to Nineveh, at least not then.

I went the other way—and I didn't walk.
I bought a ticket and got on a boat.
Everyone was working hard.
But I found a quiet cot in the bottom of the boat.
Then I put my feet up and went to sleep.

Roar! Crash! Bang! ScrEEEEch!
That's what I heard when I woke up.
Then, THUMP! (That was me falling out of bed.)
The ship jerked so hard that I couldn't stand up.
"You! Jonah!" yelled the captain.
"How can you sleep in this storm?
All hands on deck. And that means YOU!
OUT! UP!"

Black clouds boiled around a black-green sea.

Wind tore the sails to rags and drove my hair straight out in front of me.

Waves opened wide, as high as the ship.

Would the sea swallow us up--ship and all?

I looked hard into the black.

Land anywhere?

Land?

But I saw no land.

"She's leaking," someone yelled.

"Bail! Bail!" voices shouted.

We all bailed. Me too.

"She's sinking lower," came another voice.

"Throw out the cargo," ordered the captain.

We pitched basket after basket.

I helped.

The wind blew harder, and the waves got higher.

"Pray," said the captain.

Sailors fell to their knees, but they didn't know who to pray to.

I knew the real God.

But I didn't pray.

Not then.

"Who caused this storm?" a sailor asked.
Everyone looked at me.
"Me?" I asked.
"You! Jonah!"
I felt a hundred fingers pointing.
Then came their questions.
"What is your work?"
"Why are you here?"
"Who is your God?"

new I had to answer or we would all drown.

m Jonah," I said.

orship the one true God.

d made heaven.

d made the sea.

d made land."

opped and then went on.

d God made this storm."

The sailors looked in fear at the black clouds all around them.
One whispered, "What have you done?"
"God gave me a message," I said, "but I ran away."
Just then a wave slammed hard against the boat.

The sailors prayed again.
This time they prayed to my God, the true God.
"Oh, Lord God, who made the sea and sky and dry land,
please save us," they cried.

But the wind kept blowing.
I could taste saltwater in my throat.

"Please stop this storm and bring us home," they cried.
The waves whipped higher.
I could see a fish caught high in the rigging.
"We want to be Your people," they prayed.
Rain drove like needles against my eyes.
But I didn't pray.

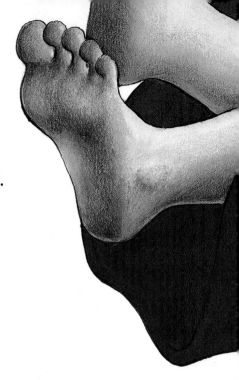

"What should we do?" the captain asked.
Suddenly, everyone got quiet.
All eyes turned toward me.

"It's my fault," I whispered to them (or to God).
"I'm sorry."
Then I said the hardest words I've ever said.
"Throw me into the water.
Then God will make the sea calm for you."

"No," they shouted.
Sailors grabbed oars and rowed harder than ever.
Still the storm roared.
Still the ship lowered in the water.
When the last sailor dropped his oars, I took a deep breath and held my nose.

The waves covered me.
At first I didn't know where I was.
The sea was strangely beautiful.
I could see sun beginning to glint on
the water surface above me.
Sun?
How could that be?
A storm raged up there.
But light slowly faded as I went down
Down.
Down.

My chest hurt.

I tried to take a breath but took in only water.

I felt seaweed around my head.

Still I went down.

It got darker and darker.

My chest hurt.

A small bright fish crossed in front of my face.

But the fish went up, and I still went down.

Down.

My chest hurt.

I must be at the bottom of undersea mountains by now.

I knew I was drowning.

Finally, I prayed.

"Help, Lord."

Nobody believes me when I tell what happened next.

I guess I don't blame them.

I've caught a lot of fish, and I know what the inside of a fish looks like.

Most fish, that is.

But just as I said, "Help," to God, I saw a shadow around me.

The shadow had teeth.

GULP!

I was inside a huge fish.

But this was not like any fish I've ever seen.

There was room in there, not just fish guts.

And air, precious air.

I gulped and gasped and sputtered and breeeeeeathed.

I wasn't drowning anymore.

But it stank, oh, did it stink.

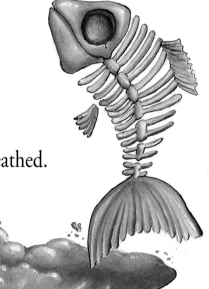

I was inside that fish a long time.
Three days, I think.
I had nothing to do.
I couldn't run anywhere.
I thought and thought.
I talked to God.
But I wondered,
*Would I ever hear God's voice again?*

Then God spoke.
But He did not speak to me.
He spoke to the fish.
The fish obeyed--
"BUUUUURRRRRRP!"
*Splat!* I flopped onto dry land.

"You! Jonah!"
"Yes, Lord?"
"Go to Nineveh."
I gathered up my coat and ran.
This time I ran toward Nineveh.

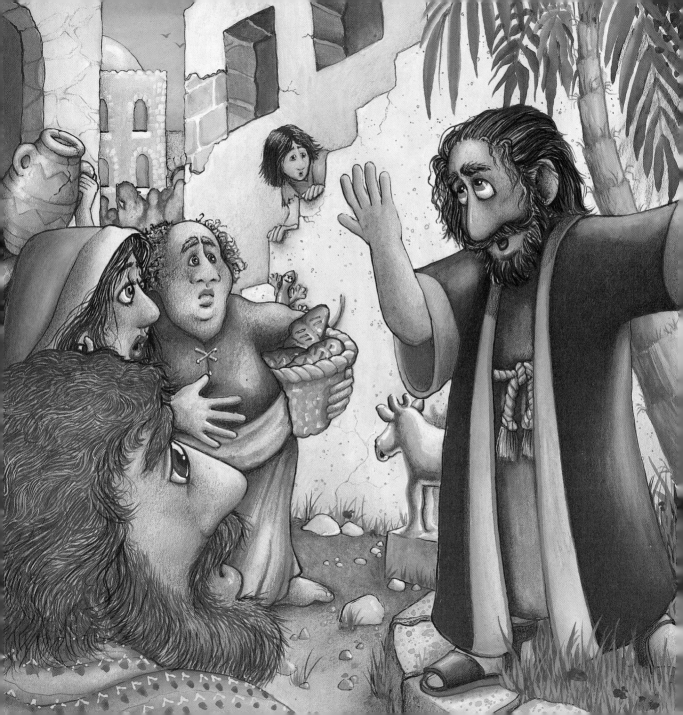

"You! Nineveh!" I shouted.
"Stop doing what is wrong.
Do what is right.
Stop hurting each other.
Stop praying to other gods.
God made heaven and sea and land."
*God made a big fish too,* I thought.
"You have forty days," I yelled.
"Shape up, or God will wipe you out!"

Then I sat up on a hill to see what would happen.
I wanted to see a dark cloud drop out of heaven.
I wanted God to blow all of Nineveh to the end of the earth.
(I still did not like the people of Nineveh.)

But Nineveh prayed to God.
People told God they were sorry for the wrongs they did.
They stopped hurting each other.

Forty days came and went.
Hot sun blistered down from heaven.
But no black cloud.

So I complained to God.
"I knew You would do this!" I shouted.
"That is why I ran away.
You are just too kind.
Why can't You stay angry?
Why do You keep on forgiving people?"

"You, Jonah," God said.
"Do you have a right to be angry?"
"Yes! Yes! Yes!" I yelled and stamped my feet.
"I have every right to be angry."

I watched and I waited day after day.
I got hot, so hot, waiting for God to get rid of Nineveh.

Nothing changed in the city.
But a big vine grew over me.
It kept me cool.
I loved the vine.

Then one morning I woke up.
The vine lay flat on the ground.
A worm peeked out its head from the stalk and laughed at me.
That day was hotter than ever.
I was madder than ever.
A burning wind whistled against my ears.

In the cool evening, God asked,
"Jonah, do you have a right to be angry?"
"I am angry enough to die," I grumbled back.
"I cared about that vine."

"But Jonah," God said in His most quiet voice.
"I care about the sailors.
I care about the people of Nineveh.
I even care about their cows.
And I care about you, Jonah."